Animals in Their Habitats

Seashore Animals

Francine Galko

Heinemann Library
Chicago, Illinois

Designed by Ginkgo Creative
Printed and bound in the United States by Lake Book Manufacturing, Inc.

07 06 05 04 03
10 9 8 7 6 5 4 3 2 1

Library of Congress Cataloging-in-Publication Data

Galko, Francine.
    Seashore animals / Francine Galko.
        p. cm. — (Animals in their habitats)
Includes bibliographical references (p.   ).
Summary: Introduces the animals that make their habitat along the
seashore.
    ISBN 1-40340-185-3 (HC), 1-4034-0442-9 (Pbk.)
    1. Seashore animals—Juvenile literature. 2. Seashore—Juvenile literature. [1. Seashore animals.] I. Title.
    QL122.2 .G25 2003
    591.769'9—dc21
                        2001007661

Acknowledgments
The author and publishers are grateful to the following for permission to reproduce copyright material:
Cover photograph by Patti Murray/Animals Animals
p. 4 Wolfgang Kaehler; p. 5 Jeff Foott/Bruce Coleman Inc.; p. 6 Rich Reid/Animals Animals; p. 7 Patricio Robles Gil/Bruce Coleman Inc.; p. 8 Jack Dermid/Bruce Coleman Inc.; p. 9 Jen and Des Bartlett/Bruce Coleman Inc.; p. 10 E. R. Degginger/Bruce Coleman Inc.; p. 11 B. G. Murray/Animals Animals; p. 12 Steinhart Aquarium/Photo Researchers, Inc.; p. 13 Joyce and Frank Burek/Animals Animals; pp. 14, 18 Patti Murray/Animals Animals; p. 15 Dwight Kuhn; p. 16 R. Jackman/OSF/Animals Animals; pp. 17, 20 Zig Leszczynski/Animals Animals; p. 19 Jim Doran/Animals Animals; p. 21 David Overcash/Bruce Coleman Inc.; p. 22 Mike Couffer/Bruce Coleman Inc.; p. 23 Bruce Watkins/Animals Animals; p. 24 M. Borland/Bruce Coleman Inc.; p. 25 John Shaw/Bruce Coleman Inc.; p. 26 Wendell Metzen/Bruce Coleman Inc.; p. 27 Trevor Barrett/Animals Animals; p. 28 John Elk III/Bruce Coleman Inc.; p. 29 Carroll Henderson
Every effort has been made to contact copyright holders of any material reproduced in this book. Any omissions will be rectified in subsequent printings if notice is given to the publisher.

Some words are shown in bold, **like this.** You can find out what they mean by looking in the glossary.

To learn more about the crab on the cover, turn to page 18.

Contents

What is a Seashore?

A seashore is a kind of **habitat**. It is the land next to the ocean. **Beaches** are seashores. Some seashores have sand or mud. There may be **seashells** on seashores.

Other seashores have rocks you can sit on.
Some have **cliffs** that rise up above the
ocean. Swimming at a rocky seashore can
be very dangerous.

Where are Seashores?

If you go to the ocean, you will see a seashore. Seashores are all over the world. They line every **continent**.

At a seashore, the **tide** comes in from the ocean every day. When the tide is in, the land is covered with water. Then the water goes back into the ocean.

Seashore Homes

Seashores have homes for many different animals. Seabirds like this tern make nests on the seashore. Terns find fish and other animals to eat in the water.

Sea lions spend most of their time in the water. They are good swimmers. Sea lions also spend time on rocky seashores. They have their babies on the seashore.

Living in the Sand

Many animals live on sandy beaches. Sand dollars use tiny **spines** to dig into the sand. They have spines all over their body.

Cockles dig into the sand. They have a
strong foot that helps them dig. People,
birds, and sea stars like to eat cockles.

Tidepools are puddles of water left behind by the **tide.** When the tide moves out, some goby fishes use suckers to hold onto a rock in the tidepool.

12

Sea lemons hold on tightly to tidepool rocks. Their bright yellow color warns **predators** away. Sea lemons taste bad!

Living on the Rocks

Barnacles cling to rocks on the seashore.
They cannot move. They wait for the waves
to bring food to them.

Sea stars can move. They are strong enough to open clam shells. Some sea stars live along rocky seashores. Others live on rocks in shallow water near the seashore.

Many animals make their home in the **shallow** water along the seashore. Jellyfish live in the water. Sometimes the **tide** brings them onto land and leaves them there.

16

All kinds of small fish live in the water
along the seashore. A butterfish feels slimy
like butter. Some people catch and eat
butterfishes.

Most crabs live in the water. But some crabs search the beach for leftover food. Sally Lightfoot crabs eat other animals and plants along the seashore.

Coquina (ko•kee•na) clams suck in the water
brought by waves. They eat tiny animals in
the water. Then they spit the water back out.

Seashore Predators

Some seashore animals are **predators.** Sea anemones use their **tentacles** to sting shrimp and fish. Then they pull the **prey** into their mouth and eat it.

Great egrets hunt prey in shallow water along seashores. They eat fishes, insects, and **shellfish.** You can see them walking in the water looking for food.

Seashore Animals' Shells

The **tide** can crush animals against rocks.
Hard shells **protect** animals from the strong
waves. This limpet makes its own shell.

22

Hermit crabs don't make their own shell. They look for an empty shell to make their home. Often hermit crabs fight over an empty shell.

Hiding at the Seashore

Camouflage is one way to hide from **predators.** Sea urchins pull rocks and shells on top of them. This helps them look like the seashore.

Can you find the fish? This tidepool sculpin looks like the sand and rocks in the water. Hiding like this is called **cryptic coloration.**

Seashore Babies

Baby brown pelicans hatch in nests on the beach or in a nearby tree. Mother pelicans bring fishes to the babies until they can swim.

Baby loggerhead turtles hatch from eggs under the sand. The young turtles have to crawl up through the sand after they hatch. Then they run into the sea and swim away.

Sometimes people build houses too close to seashores. Other people put trash or harmful chemicals on the beach. These things harm seashore animals.

We must share seashores with the animals
that live there. When you go to the seashore,
don't put trash in the water. Don't bother the
animals. Keep seashores clean and safe for
seashore animals.

Glossary

beaches land beside an ocean, sea, lake, or river

camouflage way an animal hides itself

cliff rock-like land that rises up like a mountain

continent one of the seven main pieces of land on Earth

cryptic coloration looking like something else. A fish that looks like the ocean bottom has cryptic coloration.

habitat place where an animal lives

ocean all the salt water that covers the Earth

predator animal that hunts and eats other animals

prey animal that is hunted and eaten by another animal

protect keep safe

seashell shell of an animal that lived in the ocean or sea

shallow not very deep

shellfish sea animal that lives in a shell like a clam or a mussel

spine long, thin, stick-like part of an animal's body

tentacle long part of an animal's body that is usually used to feel or hold onto things

tide movement of water from the ocean onto the land and back into the ocean. It usually happens two times each day.

tidepool puddle of water left behind by the tide

More Books to Read

Arnosky, Jim. *Crinkleroot's Guide to Knowing Animal Habitats.* New York: Aladdin Picture Books, 1998.

Gunzi, Christiane and Frank Greenaway. *Look Closer: Tide Pool.* New York: Dorling Kindersley, 1998.

Hunter, Anne. *What's in the Tidepool?* Boston: Houghton Mifflin, 2000.

Silver, Donald M. and Patricia J. Wynne. *Seashore: One Small Square.* Columbus, Ohio: McGraw-Hill, 1997.

Wallace, Karen. *DK Readers: Day at Seagull Beach.* New York: Dorling Kindersley, 1999.

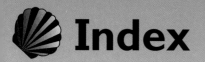

Index